The Cheese Cookbook

30 Recipes for Cheese Lovers

BY: Nancy Silverman

COPYRIGHT NOTICES

© 2019 Nancy Silverman All Rights Reserved

Subject to the agreement and permission of the author, this Book, in part or in whole, may not be reproduced in any format. This includes but is not limited to electronically, in print, scanning or photocopying.

The opinions, guidelines and suggestions written here are solely those of the Author and are for information purposes only. Every possible measure has been taken by the Author to ensure accuracy but let the Reader be advised that they assume all risk when following information. The Author does not assume any risk in the case of damages, personally or commercially, in the case of misinterpretation or misunderstanding while following any part of the Book.

My Heartfelt Thanks and A Special Reward for Your Purchase!

https://nancy.gr8.com

My heartfelt thanks at purchasing my book and I hope you enjoy it! As a special bonus, you will now be eligible to receive books absolutely free on a weekly basis! Get started by entering your email address in the box above to subscribe. A notification will be emailed to you of my free promotions, no purchase necessary! With little effort, you will be eligible for free and discounted books daily. In addition to this amazing gift, a reminder will be sent 1-2 days before the offer expires to remind you not to miss out. Enter now to start enjoying this special offer!

Table of Contents

(1) Lime Cheesecake 7

(2) Cheese Souffle, Twice–Cooked 9

(3) Warm Cheesy Fennel Dip 12

(4) Cheese and Bacon Muffins 15

(5) Taco Dipping Pots 17

(6) Cottage Cheese Dip 19

(7) Ricotta, Salami, And Sage Pizzas 21

(8) Cheese and Chicken Chimichangas 23

(9) Mini Baked Ricottas with Tomato and Basil 26

(10) Cheese and Potato Soup 29

(11) Cheesy Salmon Balls 32

(12) Cheese and Baked Bean Flat Wraps 34

(13) Feta, Rosemary, And Pumpkin Twist 36

(14) Cheese Puffs 39

(15) Chocolate Philly Loaf 41

(16) Cheese Straws 44

(17) Easy Strawberry Tiramisu 46

(18) Cheese Fondue 49

(19) Ricotta, Peas, And Basil with Pasta 52

(20) Parmesan Cheese Savoury Cheesecake 55

(21) Lemon and Blueberry Baked Cheesecake 58

(22) Fig and Goat's Cheese Tart 61

(23) Bean and Cheesy Polenta Pot Pies............................. 63

(24) Cheese, Bacon, And Olive Focaccia 66

(25) Tiramisu Mocha Cups 68

(26) Cheese and Chive Damper... 71

(27) Haloumi Hotdogs... 73

(28) Cheese and Spinach Pie 75

(29) Chilli Cheese Dip... 78

(30) Cheese and Bacon Chicken... 80

About the Author 82

Author's Afterthoughts 84

(1) Lime Cheesecake

I should just say 1 serving, because I have been known to eat the whole cake- this is so good! Just cook it up and you will see!

Preparation Time: 6 hours and 45 minutes

10 serving sizes

Ingredient List:

- 15 wheat meal biscuits of your choice
- 2 Tbsp. of butter
- 2 cups of peach and mango yogurt
- 1 tub of ricotta cheese
- 1 free range egg
- 2 tsp. of lime zest
- 2 Tbsp. of caster sugar
- ¼ cup of whole meal plain flour
- Fresh fruit, chopped

Instructions:

- Preheat oven to 370F. Grease a spring-form pan.
- Grab out your food processor and blitz biscuits to make crumbs. Add butter and combine well.
- Press crumb into base of pan, then into the fridge to set.
- Grab a bowl and electric beaters and mix yogurt, ricotta, egg, lime, sugar, and flour.
- Pour into the base and bake for 30 minutes.
- Cool to room temperature, then into the fridge.
- Serve when ready with chopped fruit… yummy!

(2) Cheese Souffle, Twice-Cooked

Delicious cheesy goodness in the form of a baked soufflé– what a great way to start your day off, or fill up with protein for lunch.

Preparation Time: 1 hour and 20 minutes

6 serving sizes

Ingredient List:

- 1 packet of vintage cheddar, grated
- 4 free-range eggs, separated
- ¾ cup of cream
- 1 tsp. of thyme leaves
- 1 tsp. of Dijon mustard
- 2 Tbsp. of butter
- 2/3 cup of plain flour
- 2 cups of milk

Instructions:

- Preheat oven to 370F. Grease 6 ramekins.
- Grab a saucepan and melt butter over a medium flame.
- Pop your flour in. Lower the flame and stir into the butter.
- Pour milk in slowly and continue stirring. A sauce will form.
- Take off the heat and add thyme, half the cheese, and mustard. Keep stirring. When cheese is melted and it's smooth, set aside to cool.
- Add yolks and combine well.
- Grab a bowl and whisk egg whites till stiff, then gently fold into yolk mixture.
- Divide into ramekins.
- Grab a baking dish big enough for 6 ramekins and fill a third of the way up with hot water.
- Pop your ramekins in, then the whole thing goes into the oven until golden and set.
- Yum!

(3) Warm Cheesy Fennel Dip

The combination of cheese and fennel is an interesting one, full of flavour! This dip is delicious and smells so amazing.

Preparation Time: 1 hour

Serving Sizes: 1 cup

Ingredient List:

- 2 fennel bulbs, sliced
- 1 brown onion, sliced
- 2 or more garlic cloves
- 2 tsp. of fennel seeds
- 1 ½ Tbsp. of parmesan cheese, grated
- 2 Tbsp. of fresh lemon juice
- 1 ½ Tbsp. of olive oil
- ½ cup of sour cream
- Crostini to serve (or crackers or corn chips or whatever you like!)

Instructions:

- Preheat oven to 390F.
- Grab out a roasting dish and pop in your fennel, onion, and garlic. Coat them in oil, cover, and roast for 40 minutes.
- Pop fennel seeds on a baking tray and roast till you can smell them. Set aside.
- Grab out your food processor and pop your roasted fennel mixture, cheese, sour cream, juice, 2/3 of the fennel seeds, and 1 Tbsp. of cold water in. Blitz until smooth.
- Pour into a serving bowl topped with fennel seeds and olive oil.

(4) Cheese and Bacon Muffins

These muffins are delicious for any time of the day, but being full of protein in the form of cheese and bacon, they really are the perfect breakfast muffins.

Preparation Time: 40 minutes

Serving Sizes: 12

Ingredient List:

- 1 cup of tasty cheese, grated
- 3 free range eggs, beaten
- 1 cup of milk
- 2 Tbsp. of butter
- 1 tsp. of olive oil
- 2 ½ cups of self-raising flour
- 2 rashers of bacon, chopped
- 2 Tbsp. of chives, chopped
- A pinch of cayenne pepper

Instructions:

- Preheat oven to 380F. Grease a 12-hole muffin tin.
- Grab a frypan and heat up oil over a high flame. Cook your bacon, then set it aside.
- Grab a bowl and pop flour, chives, bacon, cheese and pepper in.
- Pour in all wet ingredients and mix well.
- Divide into your muffin tray evenly. Put it into the oven until golden.
- They smell so good!

(5) Taco Dipping Pots

If your kids are having friends over for lunch or a movie, this is the perfect little meal for them. I love this for snacking, too, it's oh so very tasty!

Preparation Time: 20 minutes

8 serving sizes

Ingredient List:

- 2 avocados, chopped
- 2 tomatoes, diced
- ½ cup of tomato salsa
- 1 green onion, chopped finely
- 1 Tbsp. of lime juice
- ½ cup of sour cream
- 1 Tbsp. of fresh coriander, chopped
- 2 tsp. of taco seasoning
- 1 Lebanese cucumber, diced finely
- ½ cup of tasty cheese, grated
- 1 packet of corn chips

Instructions:

- Grab a bowl and mash avocado, onion, and lime together.
- Grab another bowl. Combine sour cream, coriander and seasoning.
- Grab 8 serving glasses and pop guacamole into the base of each glass. Top with salsa, sour cream over the top, then cucumber, tomato, and cheese on top. Serve up with corn chips.

(6) Cottage Cheese Dip

This is a yummy cheese dip ideal for the start of a dinner or just for snacking… Cheesy goodness at its healthiest.

Preparation Time: 30 minutes

Serving Sizes: 1 cup

Ingredient List:

- 1 tub of cottage cheese
- 1 can of cannellini beans
- 1 or more cloves of garlic
- 1-2 Tbsp. of lemon juice
- 1 tsp. of salt
- ½ tsp. of rosemary leaves, chopped
- ½ tsp. of ground black pepper
- Olive oil

Instructions:

- Grab out your food processor and pop in your garlic, salt, pepper, juice, beans, rosemary, and cheese.
- Blitz until it is smooth and creamy.
- Pop into a serving dish and drizzle with olive oil.
- Bon appetit– great with crispy vegetables.

(7) Ricotta, Salami, And Sage Pizzas

OK, I love pizza! Doesn't really even matter what's on them – I just love it! Maybe I'm part Italian? Try this delicious recipe and see what you think. Bellisimo!

Preparation Time: 20 minutes

Serving Sizes: 2

Ingredient List:

- 2 pizza bases
- 1 tub of ricotta
- 1 cup of parmesan
- 1 cup of mozzarella, grated
- 1 lemon's zest
- 2 spring onions, sliced thinly
- 1 packet of pizza salami, good quality
- Ricotta
- Sage leaves
- 2 Tbsp. of olive oil

Instructions:

- Preheat oven to 410F. Pop your pizza bases on an oven tray.
- In a bowl, mix ricotta, parmesan, and zest, then spread over bases.
- Pop mozzarella, sage, salami, spring onion and ricotta on top.
- Pour a little oil over the top.
- Into the oven for 10 minutes. When crispy, pull out and eat!

(8) Cheese and Chicken Chimichangas

Yummy Mexican goodness! Nutritious and delicious and packed with cheesiness! The family will love these…

Preparation Time: 20 minutes

4 serving sizes

Ingredient List:

- ½ an entire hot roasted chicken, shredded
- 8 soft flour tortillas
- 1 jar of taco sauce
- 1 can of refried beans
- 1 red capsicum, cut into strips
- 1 bunch of spinach
- 1 cup of cheese, grated
- ¼ cup of olive oil
- Limes
- Lettuce, shredded
- Sour cream

Instructions:

- Grab a bowl and pop your chicken and taco sauce in, and coat.
- Spread tortillas with refried beans.
- Next goes on spinach, capsicum, chicken, and cheese. Roll them up.
- Grab a fry pan.
- Heat up oil over a medium flame.
- Cook each chimichanga in the pan- they're ready when they're golden.
- Serve with lettuce, sour cream, and lime.
- YUM!!!!!

(9) Mini Baked Ricottas with Tomato and Basil

Tasty morsels of goodness that are great for lunch, lunch boxes, or just a sneaky snack. I make double the batch because they don't last long in our home...

Preparation Time: 1 hour and 30 minutes

8 serving sizes

Ingredient List:

- 8 slices of good quality prosciutto
- 8 free range eggs
- 1 packet of fresh ricotta
- 2 tomatoes, chopped
- ½ red onion, chopped
- 1 or more garlic cloves, crushed
- 2 Tbsp. of brown sugar
- ¼ cup of fresh lime juice
- 1 Tbsp. of fresh basil leaves, chopped

Instructions:

- Grab a saucepan and pop your tomato, garlic, onion, juice, and sugar in over a medium flame. Cook until sugar is dissolved.
- Bring to a boil, then lower the flame and simmer until it has thickened. Set aside.
- Preheat oven to 370F. Grease an 8-hole muffin tin.
- Grab another bowl and pop ricotta and eggs in, and whisk.
- Pour evenly into the pan, then into the oven for 20 minutes.
- Serve with tomato mix on top.
- Delicious!

(10) Cheese and Potato Soup

This is delicious and warming and really a wholesome meal. We love this winter warmer. I serve it up with garlic bread.

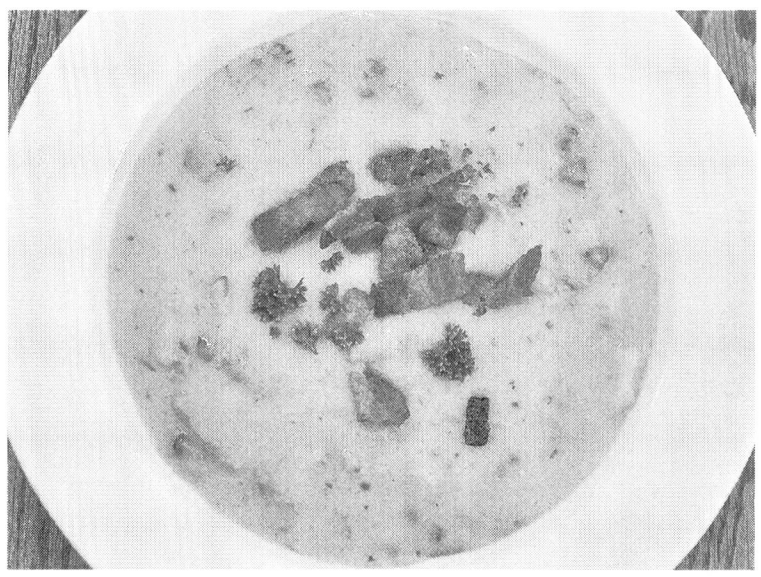

Preparation Time: 40 minutes

4 serving sizes

Ingredient List:

- 1 ½ cups of Swiss cheese, grated
- 1 bag of Desiree potatoes, chopped
- 1 Tbsp. of extra virgin olive oil
- 1 onion, chopped
- 4 cups of chicken stock
- 2 tsp. of fresh rosemary, chopped
- 1 ½ cups of milk
- 4 rashers of bacon, fried and sliced thinly
- Parmesan
- Watercress

Instructions:

- Grab a large saucepan. Heat up oil over a medium flame. Pop your onion in and cook till tender.
- Potato goes in next, then put your flame to high and pour in stock and rosemary.
- Bring to a boil, then lower flame and simmer till potato is tender.
- Let it cool, then pour into the blender, where you'll blitz till smooth and creamy.
- Stir in milk then pop back into a saucepan and heat through.
- Add cheese.
- Serve up hot, garnished with watercress, bacon, and parmesan… enjoy.

(11) Cheesy Salmon Balls

These are so good for us – packed with protein and omegas! Plus the kids love these in their lunch boxes.

Preparation Time: 35 minutes

4 serving sizes

Ingredient List:

- 1 orange sweet potato, chopped
- 1 can of salmon
- ¼ cup of cottage cheese
- 1 Tbsp. of flat-leaf parsley, chopped
- 2 Tbsp. of red onion, chopped
- 2 Tbsp. of wholemeal plain flour
- 1 Tbsp. of fresh lemon juice
- ½ cup of dried breadcrumbs

Instructions:

- Grab a saucepan and cook up sweet potato. Mash till smooth.
- Preheat oven to 370F. Grab out an oven tray. Line with baking paper.
- Grab a bowl and mix together sweet potato, cheese, juice, parsley, salmon, and flour.
- Portion into balls. Roll in breadcrumbs. Onto the baking tray.
- Into the oven until golden.

(12) Cheese and Baked Bean Flat Wraps

This is a super easy recipe that is so delicious. This is Sunday breakfast for us some days and lunch on other days– cheap and so delicious!

Preparation Time: 10 minutes

4 serving sizes

Ingredient List:

- 1 can of baked beans
- ½ cup of cheese, grated
- 4 flatbreads

Instructions:

- Grab out your sandwich press and preheat it.
- Spread baked beans over your flatbread. Sprinkle the cheese on top.
- Fold up flatbreads and onto the sandwich press till golden.
- Serve up hot!

(13) Feta, Rosemary, And Pumpkin Twist

Warm fresh bread out of the oven is one of life's best treats. Especially in the winter when you can smell it wafting through the house! Yum! Bring on winter!

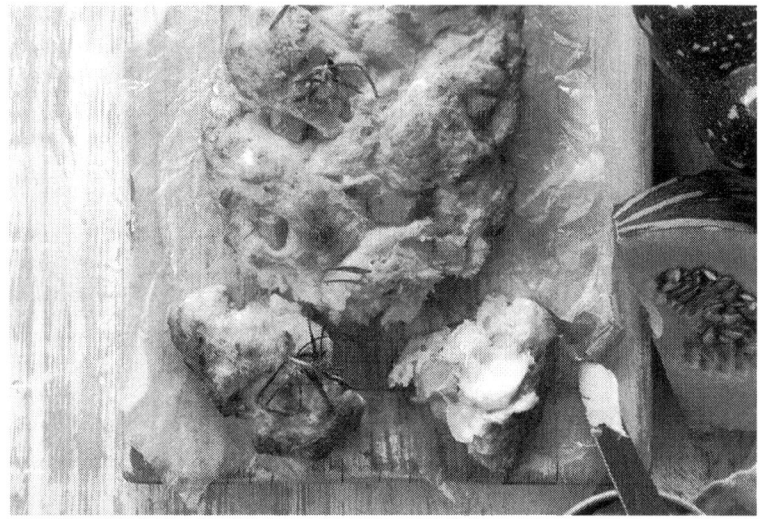

Preparation Time: 30 minutes

8 serving sizes

Ingredient List:

- 4 cups of pumpkin, steamed and chopped
- 2 cups of self-raising flour
- 1 cup of butter, chopped
- 1 packet of feta, crumbled
- 1 pinch of salt
- 1 tsp. of rosemary, chopped
- ½ cup of buttermilk
- Butter to serve

Instructions:

- Preheat oven to 410F. Grab out a baking tray and line with baking paper.
- Mash 2/3 cup of your pumpkin and set aside.
- Grab a bowl and pop your flour in with salt.
- With your hands, mix butter through until everything looks like fine breadcrumbs.
- Add mashed pumpkin, rosemary, feta, and mix.
- In the middle, pour in your milk. Using your hands, make a dough.
- Turn onto a floured surface. Knead into your desired shape. I like to plait mine.
- Push cubed pumpkin into the top. Rosemary sprigs are great on top too.
- Brush with buttermilk, then into the oven for about 20 minutes.
- Serve up hot with lashings of butter!

(14) Cheese Puffs

These tasty morsels are great when you are having a beer – a delicious snack attack for sure! Kind of naughty!

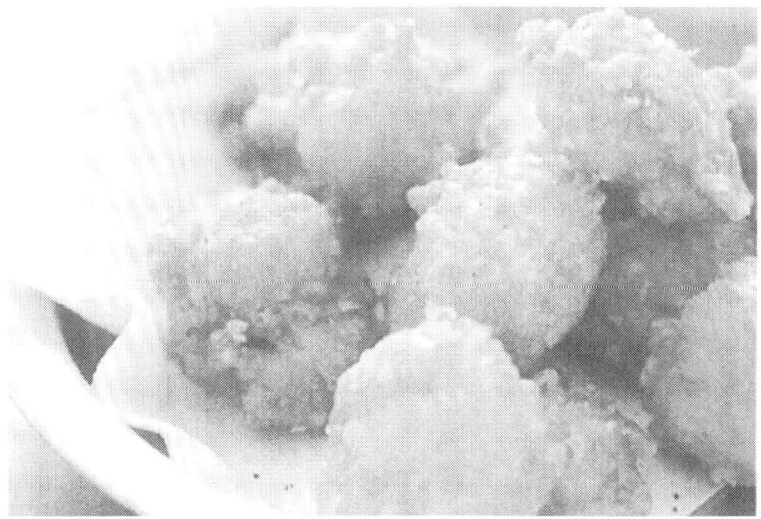

Preparation Time: 25 minutes

8 serving sizes

Ingredient List:

- 2 cups of gruyere cheese, grated
- 3 free range egg whites
- 2 ½ Tbsp. of plain flour
- Vegetable oil

Instructions:

- Grab a bowl and your electric beaters and beat egg whites till stiff and peaky.
- Gently combine with flour and cheese to make a batter.
- Grab a saucepan and fill halfway with oil. Heat over a medium flame.
- Once it's hot, drop in tsp.ful of batter.
- Preheat oven to 350F. Cook until golden. Serve hot!

(15) Chocolate Philly Loaf

This is a very moist, delicious, chocolate loaf– and I could eat the whole thing myself. Great for the kids' lunch boxes too!

Preparation Time: 1 hour and 20 minutes

8-10 serving sizes

Ingredient List:

- 1 packet of PHILADELPHIA cream cheese
- 2 free range eggs, beaten
- 1 cup of butter, softened
- 1 ¼ cups of caster sugar
- 1/3 cup of water
- 1 ¾ cups of flour
- 1 tsp. of vanilla
- 2/3 cups of cocoa
- 1 ½ tsp. of baking powder
- ½ tsp. of baking soda
- Chocolate frosting

Instructions:

- Grab out a bowl and beaters and cream the butter and sugar. Add eggs and continue to beat.
- Next goes in cream cheese, vanilla, and water.
- Fold your flour in next. Baking powder, soda, and cocoa next.
- Gently combine well, then pour into a greased loaf pan.
- Bake in oven at 370F for 1 hour.
- Let it cool, then spread frosting on top and dig in!

(16) Cheese Straws

Great for dipping in some deliciousness! Great for the lunch box too, and handy to just have in a jar for snacks!

Preparation Time: 1 hour

Serving Sizes: 30

Ingredient List:

- 1 1/3 cups of plain flour
- 1 packet of aged cheddar, grated
- ½ tsp. of salt
- ¼ tsp. of cayenne pepper
- 1 free range egg, beaten
- ½ cup of butter, chopped and chilled
- 1 Tbsp. of fresh lemon juice

Instructions:

- Preheat oven to 370F. Grab out your baking trays and line with baking paper.
- Grab a bowl and pop your flour, cayenne pepper, and salt in and mix.
- Next goes butter; rub bits of it between your fingers to disperse it until the mixture resembles breadcrumbs.
- Next goes cheese, juice, and egg. Use your hands to form a dough.
- Roll it out to desired thickness and cut into strips.
- Pop on your trays and bake till golden.
- Cheese straws ready for eating!

(17) Easy Strawberry Tiramisu

The perfect dessert when you don't have much time! It looks amazing and tastes the same!

Preparation Time: 25 minutes

4 serving sizes

Ingredient List:

- 8 sponge finger biscuits
- 1 punnet of strawberries, cut in half
- Fresh mint leaves
- 1 tub of mascarpone cheese
- 1/3 cup of marsala
- ½ tsp. of instant coffee
- 1 ½ Tbsp. of icing sugar
- ¼ cup of brown sugar
- 1 Tbsp. of boiling water

Instructions:

- Grab a bowl and pop your cheese and icing sugar in. Mix well with wooden spoon.
- In a coffee mug, combine coffee and boiling water.
- Grab out a fry pan and heat it up over a high flame. Pour in coffee, marsala, and brown sugar. Cook till sugar is dissolved.
- Lower flame to low and pop your strawberries in. Gently cook for 1 minute, then set aside.
- Pop your biscuits on plates, then pour the syrup over. Mascarpone goes on next, with strawberries and mint on top.
- Yum!!!!

(18) Cheese Fondue

One of the best things to come out of Switzerland– fondue! So fun for dinner parties, and the kids love it!

Preparation Time: about an hour

8 serving sizes

Ingredient List:

- 1 packet of gruyere cheese, grated
- 1 packet of Emmental cheese, grated
- ¼ cup of dried porcini mushrooms
- ½ a bottle of white wine
- 1 or more garlic cloves
- 1 lemon, juiced
- 2 Tbsp. of cornflour
- 1/3 cup of kirsch
- Wood fired bread, cut up into cubes

Instructions:

- Grab a bowl and soak mushrooms in hot water for about half an hour.
- Chop them up when tender.
- Grab a pan and rub your garlic around the inside of the pan, then pop the pan over a low flame.
- In go your mushrooms, lemon juice, and wine.
- Gently stir in the cheeses. When they are melted, add cornflour mixed with 3 Tbsp. of cold water.
- Add kirsch.
- Stir well, so it is creamy and smooth.
- Serve up with bread… enjoy!

(19) Ricotta, Peas, And Basil with Pasta

Quick and easy and full of good nutrition- this is a great recipe for the kids to have a go at. Take some time out to try it!

Preparation Time: 30 minutes

4 serving sizes

Ingredient List:

- 1 packet of pasta (penne is good for this recipe)
- 1 leek, thinly sliced lengthways
- ½ cup of chicken stock
- 2 cups of sugar snap peas, cut in half
- 1 cup of frozen peas
- 1 Tbsp. of olive oil
- 2 or more cloves of garlic, crushed
- ¼ cup of dill, chopped finely
- 1 cup of basil leaves
- 1 packet of ricotta cheese, crumbled
- Crusty bread

Instructions:

- Grab a saucepan and cook up your pasta. Drain and set aside.
- Grab a fry pan and heat up your oil over a medium flame. Cook your garlic and leek until tender.
- Add stock and bring to a boil, then pop your dill, peas, and sugar snaps in.
- Cook for 1 minute, then take off the heat and add your pasta, cheese, and basil.
- Combine gently.
- Season and serve.

(20) Parmesan Cheese Savoury Cheesecake

Yum! Try this recipe– you will be delighted. Puts a little spin on your regular cheesecake recipe… Simply delicious!

Preparation Time: about an hour

8 serving sizes

Ingredient List:

- 1 box of Jatz biscuits, crushed
- 6 rashers of your favourite bacon, chopped finely
- 3 Tbsp. of butter
- 1 tub of fresh ricotta cheese
- 1 tub of cream cheese
- 1 ¼ cups of parmesan, grated
- 1 onion, chopped finely
- 4 free range eggs, beaten

Instructions:

- Preheat oven to 350F and grease your spring-form pan. Line with baking paper.
- Grab a bowl and pour in biscuits and butter, and mash together with your hands.
- Press into your pan base and pop it in the freezer till it firms up.
- Grab your fry pan. Cook your onion and bacon over a medium flame. Set it aside.
- Grab out your food processor and combine eggs, cheeses, 1 cup of parmesan, and season with salt and pepper.
- Blitz till smooth, then pop into a bowl and add your bacon.
- Pour into the pan over the biscuit base.
- Sprinkle with parmesan.
- Pop into the oven for 45 minutes.
- Serve slightly cooled– yum!

(21) Lemon and Blueberry Baked Cheesecake

So very delicious and it looks amazing at the same time! This is a great one to pull out for a dinner party!

Preparation Time: 7 hours and 30 minutes

6 serving sizes

Ingredient List:

- 1 tub of cream cheese, softened
- 2 cups of cream
- 1 ½ cups of fresh frozen blueberries
- ¾ cup of caster sugar
- 3 free range eggs
- 1 tsp. of lemon zest
- 2 Tbsp. of lemon juice
- 1 tsp. of vanilla extract
- 2 cups of Scotch finger biscuits
- 3 Tbsp. of butter
- Fresh berries, to decorate
- Icing sugar, to dust

Instructions:

- Preheat oven to 360F and grease a spring-form pan, then line with baking paper.
- Grab out your food processor and pop your biscuits in. Blitz.
- Butter goes in next. Blitz.
- Press crumbs into pan to form a base. Into the fridge to chill.
- Clean out processor, then pop your cheese, zest, sugar, half your cream, and the vanilla in. Blitz till creamy. Pop your eggs in one at a time and mix between each addition.
- Pour into your pan with half the berries on top.
- Into the oven for 1 hour.
- Cool and refrigerate.
- Dust with icing sugar when you are ready to serve.
- Pop some whipped cream and remaining berries on top – so good!

(22) Fig and Goat's Cheese Tart

Gourmet tart for lunch anyone? This is a scrumptious combination and I could eat the whole tart myself! Try it out!

Preparation Time: 30 minutes

4 serving sizes

Ingredient List:

- 4 fresh ripe figs, sliced lengthways thickly
- 2 packets of goat's cheese
- 2 sheets of puff pastry
- 2 Tbsp. of raw honey, local and unprocessed

Instructions:

- Preheat oven to 390F. Grab out a baking tray and line with baking paper.
- Pop one pastry sheet down on the tray. Take the second sheet and use it to make a border around the first.
- Spread half of your goat's cheese on the pastry sheet. Pop your figs on top. Crumble the rest of your cheese over the top and pour honey all over.
- Into the oven for 15 minutes.
- It will smell amazing and taste even better.

(23) Bean and Cheesy Polenta Pot Pies

So delicious and super easy to make– these tasty pot pies are filling and so very nutritious!

Preparation Time: 45 minutes

4 serving sizes

Ingredient List:

- 1 can of Heinz Beanz Creations– Spanish
- 2 zucchinis, diced
- 1 tomato, chopped
- 1 capsicum, diced
- 1 onion, chopped finely
- 1 Tbsp. of olive oil
- 1 Tbsp. of oregano, chopped
- 1 ½ cups of water
- ½ cup of instant polenta
- 1 Tbsp. of butter
- ½ cup of mozzarella, grated

Instructions:

- Grab a fry pan and heat up oil over a medium flame.
- Cook onion till tender, then increase flame and pop in your capsicum, zucchini, and tomato.
- Cook till tender, then add beanz and oregano.
- Grab a saucepan and boil water over a high flame. Pour in polenta and stir continuously.
- Reduce flame and simmer. When polenta is soft, add butter and cheese and stir until smooth and creamy.
- Preheat a grill with a medium flame.
- Grab 4 ramekins and divide your vegetables among them.
- Pop your polenta on top, then cook under the grill till golden.
- Enjoy!

(24) Cheese, Bacon, And Olive Focaccia

This is a delicious lunch washed down with a glass of white wine– one of my favourite easy lunch dishes. Cheesy goodness at its Italian best!

Preparation Time: 40 minutes

2 serving sizes

Ingredient List:

- 1 ½ cups of mozzarella cheese
- 2 pieces of focaccia bread
- 2 Tbsp. of Kalamata olives, pitted
- 4 rashers of your favourite bacon, halved crossways
- 1/3 cup of tomato relish
- Basil leaves

Instructions:

- Preheat your grill to a medium flame and grill bacon to your liking.
- Spread relish on your focaccia, then pop half the portioned cheese on top.
- Next goes bacon and olives, then the rest of the cheese on top.
- Pop it on a tray and under the grill till golden.
- Basil leaves on top and serve up hot… with wine please!

(25) Tiramisu Mocha Cups

This is totally naughty but so very delicious! This is a gorgeous recipe you will adore, and keep going back for more…

Preparation Time: 50 minutes

Serving Sizes: 6

Ingredient List:

- 1 ½ cups of strong black coffee, cooled
- 1 ½ Tbsp. of Kahlua
- 3 cups of cantuccini biscuits
- 1 tub of mascarpone
- 2 cups of double thick chocolate custard
- 1/3 cup of thickened cream
- 2 Tbsp. of icing sugar mix
- 2 tsp. of vanilla bean paste
- Chocolate covered coffee beans, to serve
- Chocolate shards, to serve

Instructions:

- Grab a bowl and mix the Kahlua and coffee.
- Grab half the biscuits and dip into the coffee mixture.
- Divide the biscuits between six serving glasses as you go.
- Grab another bowl and mix together mascarpone, vanilla, icing sugar, and cream.
- Portion it into your glasses.
- Grab the rest of your biscuits.
- Dip in Kahlua mixture and pop into your glasses on top of everything else.
- Pour your custard into the glasses, then into the fridge to chill for 30 minutes.
- Top with coffee beans and chocolate.

(26) Cheese and Chive Damper

This delicious bread goes well with most meals – we like to sop up the gravy from our roast with this tasty cheesy bread!

Preparation Time: 55 minutes

6 serving sizes

Ingredient List:

- 2 ½ cups of self-raising flour
- 1 cup of cheddar, grated
- 1 tsp. of baking powder
- 1 ¼ cups of buttermilk
- 1 free range egg
- 1 bunch of chives, chopped

Instructions:

- Preheat oven to 370F.
- Grab a bowl and mix together flour, cheddar, baking powder, and chives.
- Pop an egg in the middle and combine into a dough.
- Turn it out onto a floured surface and knead. Shape it into your desired shape, and pop it on a baking-paper-lined baking tray.
- Into the oven until golden. Let it rest for 5 minutes if you can, then serve it up hot!
- Your family will love you forever!

(27) Haloumi Hotdogs

This is a cheesy vegetarian delight— with a spicy little kick. You never know, it might just replace the humble frankfurt!

Preparation Time: 35 minutes

4 serving sizes

Ingredient List:

- 3 cups of mixed vegetables, sliced thickly (whatever you fancy)
- 4 crispy hot dog buns or baguettes
- 1 packet of haloumi
- 1 avocado, smashed
- 1 Tbsp. of fresh herbs, chopped (your choice – I love basil)
- Sweet chilli sauce
- 1 ½ tsp. of fresh lime juice

Instructions:

- Preheat a barbecue grill over a medium flame.
- Coat your vegetables in olive oil, then chargrill and set aside.
- Pop your buns on the chargrill. Pop your haloumi on next and char for 1 minute each side- smells so good.
- Pour your lime juice on the haloumi.
- Grab a bowl and mix juice, avocado, and fresh herbs.
- Spread over buns.
- Pop your haloumi, vegetables, and sweet chilli sauce in… So very tasty!

(28) Cheese and Spinach Pie

This is a very tasty combination. The beauty of cooking with cheese – is you know that it is full of protein and so very good for you!

Preparation Time: 35 minutes

4 serving sizes

Ingredient List:

- 8 sheets of filo pastry, halved crossways
- 8 sprigs of fresh flat-leaf parsley
- 1 bunch of English spinach, chopped
- 1 tub of fresh ricotta
- 1 tub of kefalotyri cheese
- 2 free range eggs
- 2 ripe tomatoes, chopped
- 2 Tbsp. of olive oil
- 2 or more garlic cloves, crushed
- 1 Tbsp. of fresh oregano, chopped
- 1 Tbsp. of fresh flat-leaf parsley, chopped

Instructions:

- Preheat oven to 410F and grease four ramekins.
- Grab a saucepan, pop your spinach in, and cook till it wilts. Take off the heat and drain.
- Grab a bowl and combine cheeses, eggs, herbs, and garlic.
- Add your spinach and gently mix.
- Into your ramekins goes 4 pieces of filo. Brush each with oil, then pour spinach mixture in.
- Into the oven for 15 minutes.
- Serve up with tomatoes and parsley… delicious!

(29) Chilli Cheese Dip

I find it so hard not to start spooning this dip into my gob after making it– it is so delicious and moreish! Enjoy!

Preparation Time: 20 minutes

Serving Sizes: 2 cups

Ingredient List:

- I tub of cream cheese
- 2 tsp. of oil
- 1 cup of baby spinach leaves, chopped
- 1 red onion, chopped finely
- 1 or more garlic cloves, crushed (the more garlic the better)
- 2 tomatoes, diced
- ¼ cup of sweet chilli sauce
- 2 Tbsp. of fresh chives, chopped
- Paprika

Instructions:

- Grab a large fry pan and heat oil over a high flame. Cook onions until tender, then pop your tomatoes and spinach in and cook until wilted.
- Lower the flame.
- Add chives, chilli, and cream cheese.
- When smoothly combined, pop into a serving bowl.
- Serve warm with corn chips… so tasty!

(30) Cheese and Bacon Chicken

Cheese and bacon and chicken together is a dream come true for my little girl. This recipe always puts a smile on her face. So tasty!

Preparation Time: 45 minutes

1 serving

Ingredient List:

- 1 chicken breast
- 1 slice of Swiss cheese, quartered
- 2 small potatoes, quartered
- 3 tsp. of olive oil
- 2 rashers of your favourite bacon, halved lengthways
- 2 baby squash, quartered and steamed
- 1 carrot, sliced and steamed

Instructions:

- Preheat oven to 420F.
- Coat potatoes with oil and pop in a baking dish. Roast till golden.
- Meanwhile, cut a pocket into your chicken and pop your cheese in.
- Wrap your chicken in bacon. Toothpicks can secure the bacon.
- Grab out a fry pan and heat oil over a medium flame.
- Cook your chicken for 1 minute each side, then pop it in the oven with potatoes.
- Roast till the chicken is cooked through and serve up with steamed squash and carrots. Yum!

About the Author

Nancy Silverman is an accomplished chef from Essex, Vermont. Armed with her degree in Nutrition and Food Sciences from the University of Vermont, Nancy has excelled at creating e-books that contain healthy and delicious meals that anyone can make and everyone can enjoy. She improved her cooking skills at the New England Culinary Institute in Montpelier Vermont and she has been working at perfecting her culinary style since graduation. She claims that her life's work is always a work in progress and she only hopes to be an inspiration to aspiring chefs everywhere.

Her greatest joy is cooking in her modern kitchen with her family and creating inspiring and delicious meals. She often says that she has perfected her signature dishes based on her family's critique of each and every one.

Nancy has her own catering company and has also been fortunate enough to be head chef at some of Vermont's most exclusive restaurants. When a friend suggested she share some of her outstanding signature dishes, she decided to add cookbook author to her repertoire of personal achievements. Being a technological savvy woman, she felt the e-book realm would be a better fit and soon she had her first cookbook available online. As of today, Nancy has sold over 1,000 e-books and has shared her culinary experiences and brilliant recipes with people from all over the world! She plans on expanding into self-help books and dietary cookbooks, so stayed tuned!

Author's Afterthoughts

Thank you for making the decision to invest in one of my cookbooks! I cherish all my readers and hope you find joy in preparing these meals as I have.

There are so many books available and I am truly grateful that you decided to buy this one and follow it from beginning to end.

I love hearing from my readers on what they thought of this book and any value they received from reading it. As a personal favor, I would appreciate any feedback you can give in the form of a review on Amazon and please be honest! This kind of support will help others make an informed choice on and will help me tremendously in producing the best quality books possible.

My most heartfelt thanks,

Nancy Silverman

If you're interested in more of my books, be sure to follow my author page on Amazon (can be found on the link Bellow) or scan the QR-Code.

https://www.amazon.com/author/nancy-silverman

Printed in Poland
by Amazon Fulfillment
Poland Sp. z o.o., Wrocław